D0173746

TABLE OF CONTENTS

Introduction

It sounds like an impossible task: Write an essay that reveals exactly who you are, makes you sound brilliant and humble at the same time, and stands out from the other gazillion applicants. Also, tell your unique, compelling story using masterful writing skills no one ever taught you. And don't forget to fit it all in under the word count.

Welcome to Essay Hell.

Don't worry. Everyone is in the same boat. Most students dread them. Some stall as long as possible. Others start early. A few freak out. The trick is to stay calm, and make a plan. Essays that are supposed to be about you—called "personal statements"—have been around forever. Most are written in a first-person, storytelling style that's called narrative writing.

Many books on the market can teach you all about the art of narrative writing and college application essays. But who has the time? The good news is there is a simple formula you can follow to write a standout, slice-of-life narrative essay. And it doesn't have to take weeks and months. I call it the Show *and* Tell approach. It's simple to learn and follow, and even easy to expand, change and take in many different directions.

Escape Essay Hell!

A Step-by-Step Guide
To Writing Narrative
College Application Essays

By Janine Robinson

Escape Essay Hell! will help you find a terrific topic—which is half the battle—and then step you through the process of finding a memorable story that you can use to Show *and* Tell about yourself. By following my 10 easy steps, you will be out of Essay Hell in no time!

This Guide Works for Most Application Essays

The 10 steps in *Escape Essay Hell!* are designed to help you write narrative essays for almost any prompt or question on a college, post-college or scholarship application that requires you to write about yourself. The wording of the prompts (or essay questions) can vary, but you can use this Show *and* Tell approach if they want you to: tell about yourself, an experience, accomplishment, incident, talent, story, a "time," event, life experience, obstacle, contribution, failure, achievement, family circumstance, etc.

Look for key phrases, such as, "We want to learn about you" or "Write an essay that conveys who you are."

What exactly is a narrative essay? It's when you tell a true, real-life story that happened to you, but it reads like fiction. This storytelling style is similar to something you would read in a novel, memoir or short story. Unlike formal, academic essays, these can be engaging and fun to read—which is exactly what you want in a college application essay.

Here are common prompts that this guide can help you respond to or answer:

1. The Common Application prompts. Five new prompts were introduced in 2013-14. This guide works best for answering the first two questions, although it could be tweaked for any of them.

2. The University of California Application: This guide is perfect to help you answer Prompt #2: "Tell us about a personal quality, talent, accomplishment, contribution or experience that is important to you."

3. Many Other State Universities: Although the prompts can change from year to year, many public universities that do not use The Common App ask for essays where you write about yourself.

4. Supplemental Essays ("Supps"): Since The Common App dropped its only supplemental essay requirement in 2013, many of its member schools have added their own additional prompts, or supplemental essay requirements. Many are looking for personal statement type of essays to learn more about you.

5. Other Types of Application Essays: This guide is perfect if you need to write a personal statement (or about yourself) to apply for a scholarship, a special program (like a film, art, cooking or music school) or graduate school (law, medical, business, etc.).

6. Applications Where It's Not Helpful: This guide is not as useful if you are answering a prompt or question on a college application that has a specific question it wants you to answer. For example, if it gives you a famous quote to respond to, or asks why you want to attend a certain college, or why you have chosen a certain major or field of study. Although the general Show *and* Tell approach can be applied to many questions, you would need to shape your essay to make sure it addressed the details of the prompts.

Why Trust Me?

For the last six years, I have tutored college-bound students and other clients on how to write their application essays.

Most of my students have been bright, high achievers, and yet many struggled to understand how to write their college essays. The main reason is that English classes rarely teach narrative writing.

As a former journalist, professional writer and English teacher, I help students brainstorm strong topic ideas, and then counsel them on how to write personal, slice-of-life narratives that reveal their personalities and character. Although I cannot take credit for their success, most of my students have been accepted to their top choice colleges.

Most college admissions "experts" will give you lots of advice on how to write a great essay. They say things like, "Tell a story," or "Make sure your essay is about YOU," or "Be an individual." And they are correct. But no one ever explains exactly **how** to do that. Until now!

This guide is written as though I'm sitting next to you as your personal writing coach, directing and cheering you through the process. If you spend an hour or so a day on these, you can have them done in less than a week. You can even crank out a killer rough draft in one sitting.

The QUICKIE Guide

If you don't think you need to read through all 10 steps, and want to skip right to the most basic instructions, you can use the QUICKIE notes, which are the first paragraph or two at the top of each step in **bold**. If you get stumped on any step and want further guidance or explanation, just keep reading that chapter.

If You Follow All Ten Steps, You Can Expect An Essay That:

- Grabs the reader with an engaging story.

- Reveals something unique about you.
- Reads like a piece of fiction.
- Showcases your best qualities in a humble way.
- Uses a casual writing style perfect for these essays.
- Conveys your unique voice and point of view.
- Shows the reader how you think and what you value.

What are we waiting for? Let's start your escape now!

Step One:
Find Your Defining Qualities

QUICKIE: Write down three to five, or more, of your defining or core qualities or characteristics. Examples: Determined, creative, insightful, sarcastic, logical, respectful, humble, bold, etc. Pick one or two that stand out over the others.

Pull out a piece of paper (or open a new computer file). You are going to jot down about five "defining qualities" about yourself. What's a defining quality? One way to find yours is to think of how your parents or friends might describe you to someone who doesn't know you. "John, why, he's a really *determined* guy, who has a lot of *focus* and *self-discipline*. Sometimes he can be a bit *stubborn*..."

There you go; five defining qualities right there. Note that even "bad" qualities can be worth including if they are a big part of who you are—and have an "up" side. For example, even if you are stubborn, it could come in handy if it means you stick to a goal.

You might wonder: Why should I pick just one defining quality to write about myself, when I have many good ones? By sticking to just one, your essay will naturally have a sharp focus. This is a good thing. The worst essays are usually the ones that are too general and broad.

HOT TIP: Also, if you are one of those students who already has a strong idea of what field of study you intend to pursue, it helps to identify which of your core qualities would make you effective.

Here's the long list. You should be able to find a few good ones here:

Able, Accepting, Accurate, Achieving, Adaptable, Adorable, Adventurous, Affectionate, Alert, Altruistic, Ambitious, Analytical, Appreciative, Appealing, Artistic, Assertive, Attentive, Authentic, Aware, Balanced, Beautiful, Blissful, Bold, Brave, Calm, Capable, Careful, Carefree, Caring, Cautious, Centered, Certain, Charitable, Charming, Cheeky, Cheerful, Civic-Minded, Clean, Colorful, Competitive, Clear-Thinking, Communicative, Compassionate, Compatible, Competitive, Complete, Confident, Conscientious, Considerate, Conservative, Consistent, Content, Co-operative, Courageous, Courteous, Creative, Cuddly, Curious, Cultural, Cute, Decisive, Deliberate, Delicate, Delightful, Dependable, Desirable, Determined, Devoted, Disciplined, Discrete, Discriminating, Dynamic, Easy-Going, Eager, Efficient, Elegant, Empathetic, Enduring, Energetic, Enlightened, Enthusiastic, Entrepreneurial, Exciting, Experienced, Fair-Minded, Faithful, Farsighted, Fast-learner, Feeling, Fierce,

Flexible, Flourishing, Focused, Forgiving, Fortuitous, Free, Friendly, Frugal, Funny, Generous, Gentle, Good, Glorious, Graceful, Gratuitous, Great, Groovy, Happy, Harmonious, Healthy, Helpful, Holistic, Hopeful, Humble, Humorous, Honest, Humble, Idealistic, Imaginative, Integrity, Independent, Individualistic, Industrious, Innovative, Insightful, Inspirational, Interesting, Intelligent, Intense, Intuitive, Inventive, Invigorating, Joyful, Just, Kind, Leader, Learned, Loving, Loyal, Lucky, Luscious, Luxurious, Macho, Magical, Magnificent, Masculine, Mature, Moral, Motivating, Natural, Neat, Needed, Nurturing, Obedient, Objective, Open, Optimistic, Original, Organized, Outgoing, Outstanding, Passionate, Patient, Peaceful, Perceptive, Persevering, Persistent, Persuasive, Playful, Poetic, Polite, Popular, Powerful, Practical, Precious, Precise, Profound, Progressive, Proud, Professional, Punctual, Pure, Purposeful, Questioning, Quick-witted, Realistic, Reliable, Resilient, Resourceful, Respectful, Responsible, Rich, Romantic, Seductive, Selfless, Self-Aware, Self-Confident, Self-Disciplined, Sensitive, Serene, Sharp, Sincere, Smooth, Soft, Spiritual, Spontaneous, Stable, Steadfast, Strategic, Strong, Strong-willed, Stylish, Successful, Supportive, Sympathetic, Tactful, Talented, Tasty, Tenacious, Tender, Terrific, Thinking, Thorough, Thoughtful, Thrifty, Thriving, Tolerant, Tough, Trusting, Trustworthy, Unassuming, Understanding, Unwavering, Uplifting, Useful, Valuable, Verbal, Vibrant, Vital, Warm, Wholesome, Willing, Wise, Worthy.

You can also use short phrases, if single words don't nail it: Shy, but likes to be in front of an audience; conservative, but knows when to take a risk; unorganized, but highly creative; quiet, but passionate; talkative, but knows when to keep quiet; logical, but an original thinker ...

Now that you have a short list of core qualities, we are going to select one at a time and start trolling your past for "the times" or moments when you either 1) **displayed** that quality, 2) **developed** that quality, or 3) **tested** that quality. Once you find "a time" to go along with a defining quality, you probably also have a story—and a potential essay topic!

Why are these so important? If your story springs from one of your defining qualities, it will automatically reveal a large part of what makes you unique and will set you apart from the pack.

Step Two:
Search for "A Time"

QUICKIE: Think of "a time" when you displayed, developed or tested one of your defining qualities. You are looking for a real-life example of your quality that you can describe in a mini-story, also called an anecdote. This will be used as your introduction. Write down the details in story form. Tell the reader what happened during this moment, interaction or event.

Pick one of your defining qualities. Think back over the last few years to find "times" when you used that quality, or when it played a role in something that happened to you. You are looking for those moments, experiences, incidents, mini-stories from your past. Often these incidents are times when that quality was challenged somehow, or strengthened, shaped, or first tested.

Write down your ideas next to each quality. (These are just notes at this point.) Even if you think, "There's no way that would make a good essay," write it down anyway. These "times" do not need to be the highlights, the victories, the major accomplishments in your life. In fact, the more simple, ordinary and everyday, the better (more on the amazing power of "mundane" topics later.) You might be surprised.

This is what you are looking for: The TIME I was determined…and baked a dozen banana cream pies until I got them just right. The TIME I was creative…and made a hanging mobile using junk I found at the beach. The TIME I was a leader…and walked a group of disabled kids down a mountain during a thunderstorm. They will be little moments or experiences that often lasted no longer than a few minutes to a half hour, which will serve as real-life examples of your defining quality.

Here are some great places to search your brain for memorable "times":

> **Extra-curricular activities**: dance, yoga, pool, surfing, hiking, foosball, …
> **Hobbies**: chess, video games, rock collecting, cutting hair, gardening, …
> **Summer jobs**: washing dishes, ushering, bagging groceries, babysitting, …
> **Family activities**: cooking, camping, playing cards, arguing, driving, …
> **Summer camp:** sailing, camping, making fires, using a compass, …
> **Trips:** camp outs, big cities, mission trips, volunteer activities, …
> **Time with friends**: at the beach, watching movies, eating yogurt, learning to drive, …
> **School clubs**: Spanish, Future Farmers of America, chess, environmental, …

Your bedroom: posters on your wall, knickknacks on your dresser, souvenirs on the shelves, books on nightstand, …

The Internet: photos in your Facebook page, bookmarks in your browser, favorite lists from Tumbler, Instagram favorites, your blogs, …

HOT TIP: I already suggested that you keep an eye out for defining qualities that would make you effective in your future schooling plans. (It's not necessary, however, if you don't know yet.) For example, if you know you want to be a doctor and are starting as a biology major, it wouldn't hurt to look for qualities you think would make you an effective doctor—empathy, precision, ambition, drive, etc. If you think you will go into engineering, find qualities that could help your career—problem-solver, logical thinker, curiosity, dogged, a tinkerer, etc. Or a future in the arts—creative, expressive, visionary, passionate, disciplined, etc.

Your friends—and especially your parents—can help you identify both your "defining qualities" and related "times," or examples of them. They can help you think back over your past to find those little moments, interactions, incidents, highlights or dramas in your life. (Ideally, you want to find "times" that happened during your high school years, and not go too far back into your childhood.) Often, they remember little stories or interesting things that happened to you that you have forgotten. Pull out photo albums to spark ideas, or just sit them down and ask directly. Most parents, as you know, are eager to help.

Another Approach

Another way to find a great anecdote and topic is to first brainstorm those funny, odd, interesting, memorable, moving, silly, unforgettable "times" from your recent past—and then look for the defining quality you used, developed or had tested during that experience. The goal is to find "a time" that was connected in some meaningful way to a core part of who you are. You just start looking for it from a different angle.

HOT TIP: Parents can be a big help with these essays, but sometimes they can get in the way of you finding and telling a really great story. The problem is that many still believe you need to impress college admissions officers, and they don't trust that story-based essays do that the best way. Try your best to enlighten them!

One of the biggest mistakes students make when picking topics is think they need to find impressive ones. It's counter-intuitive (not what you would think), but "times," stories or topics that involve basic, everyday "mundane" situations make the best essays.

Examples of Mundane Topics

Washing cars, scooping ice-cream, pulling weeds, building a go-cart, singing karaoke, a broken thumb, frizzy hair, big feet, riding public busses, bee allergies, your TX11 calculator, playing Bananagrams, fixing old radios, learning to drive a stick shift, making crepes, tying knots, etc.

HOT TIP: **Great Accomplishments = Dull Essays**

The worst thing you can do with an essay is try to impress the reader. Even though you probably feel intense pressure to do this, flaunting your accomplishments is not the goal of these essays. You do not need a SUPER topic—such as The Time You Climbed Mount Everest or How You Won the National Chess Tournament—to write a great story. (College admissions counselors will see how fabulous you are in other parts of the application.) In fact, anything that even hints of bragging can make you sound unlikable.

Topics to Avoid

My amazing mission trip; The time we won the state championship; Life as a chair-one violinist; Making the lead in the school play; Earning my Eagle Scout. There can be wonderful topics *within* these broader achievements, but focus on the more specific moments. For instance, look for something interesting, unusual or significant that happened *while* you were on the mission trip, instead of just writing about the mission trip itself. That way, the mission trip will be in the background of your essay, and the engaging story will be the featured element.

An everyday topic is more powerful than an "impressive" one because the mundane is naturally more interesting to read about, and reveals your grounded, humble and likable character. If you write about a huge accomplishment, you're at risk of sounding self-impressed (even if you're not). And frankly, these types of "amazing feats" stories just aren't that interesting. Do you like hearing about other people's big winning moments? Or do you prefer hearing about times things went a bit sideways, and how they recovered?

Once you dig up some "times," try to find ones in the strangely appealing world of the mundane. Don't rule anything out.

Step Three:
Choose the Right Story

QUICKIE: To ensure that you have a compelling mini-story (an anecdote) for your introduction that will grab the reader, check to see that it involves some type of "problem." Problems come in all forms, such as a crisis, accident, challenge, failure, change, obstacle, personal flaw, phobia, major change, mistake, etc. If your story involves a problem, chances are it will be interesting to read—which is exactly what you want.

By this step, you should have a defining quality that you want to explore, and some examples or little stories, incidents or moments involving that quality. Now it's time to dig a little deeper and pick your best story—the one that will hook the reader right at the start and keep them reading until the last word.

There's a trick to this—and it works every time!

Do you remember from your English classes what makes a story? No matter what, you need two things: a character(s) and a conflict. With these essays, you are the main character. To find an irresistible story, all you need to find is a conflict. If the "time," incident or example you already thought of has a conflict, chances are it will make a good story, and essay! Let's run it through the test. If not, you just need to look harder.

Why You Want a Juicy Problem

What's a conflict? It's nothing more than a **problem**. These come in all shapes and sizes. The problem you describe does not need to be a disaster, tragedy or a life-threatening crisis (although those can work, too.) The problem often is something that got in the way of whatever you wanted to do, or try, or valued. It can be an obstacle, either literally or figuratively, such as an accident, mistake, life change, big move, disappointment, failure, or any setback in your life. It also can be an obsession, passion, phobia, challenge or even a seemingly impossible goal. Or it can be a personal idiosyncrasy, such as a bad habit, physical flaw or difference. One guy wrote about his crazy, frizzy red hair. Another girl wrote about her wide hips.

Once you find a problem that relates to one of your defining qualities, you will also reveal a relevant, compelling story to tell. And *voila*, you have your topic. Not to confuse you, but sometimes your defining quality can actually be the problem, such as someone with a temper or bad habit. Usually the "defining quality or characteristic" will be what helped you handle the problem, such as being resourceful, self-disciplined or persistent.

If you can find a problem, you will have an interesting story. Why does that automatically make your story readable and compelling? Because admit it or not, everyone loves a juicy problem. Don't you? Think about your favorite movie, book, or story you like to tell your friends. Bet it involved a problem. So with these essays, problems are a good thing.

Describing a problem, and then explaining how you handled it, will produce a compelling essay. Admissions officers use these admissions essays to see how you think, what you care about and how you learn in order to decide if you would be a good fit for their school or program. (Some even use them to help determine how much scholarship money to give you.)

I always advise my students to read sample essays to spark ideas for their own topics. Especially when it comes to mundane topics, they need to see examples to believe they make great essays.

Sample Topics

See if some of these topics from former students will open your thinking to the possibilities of your own unique topic:

- The girl who starred in all the school musicals, but wrote about her obsession with karaoke.

- The boy who was 6-foot-5 and 300 pounds and didn't like how other kids often thought he was mean.

- The girl who tried to loose weight to reduce her wide hips, but realized it was a family trait that represented positive qualities, such as stability and strength.

- The boy who forgot to water his dad's prized plumeria plants while away on vacation because he got caught up in a week of surfing.

- The girl from a small beach town who got separated from her family on a trip to Barcelona, but how that scare didn't stop her determination to be a city girl.

- The boy who wrote about how he loved technology so much that he always held off buying the latest iPhone or computers because of the promise of a newer model—and always had outdated gadgets.

- The boy who loved to collect other people's junk—even dragging home an old trampoline—and why he valued his "prizes."

- The girl who was such a perfectionist that she made her bed before getting into it every night, and how she endured a family of slobs.

- The boy who loved tying knots but got stuck in a tree because he tied the wrong knot, and how this related to his overall problem-solving skills.

- The girl who wrote about her lifelong obsession with yellow, from her bedroom wallpaper to her Halloween costumes to her first car, and how that reflected her positive outlook, and also her gentle, insightful nature.

- The boy who mixed up someone's food order while waiting tables and had to pay for a family's entire meal, and learned to swallow his pride.

- The girl who worked as a golf caddie and how she realized the other boy caddies never invited her to join them for lunch.

- The injured boy who started singing a rock song lying on a gurney in the ER to calm himself, and how other patients chimed in.

Starting to get the idea? Most of these topics sprung from basic stories, usually involving some type of a problem. Of course, what made their essays great was what they had to say about these topics.

What I love is that you can almost imagine how the college admissions officers who read these essays would dub or nickname the writers to remember them: The kid who got stuck in the tree; the kid who sang songs in the ER; the kid who loved yellow; the city girl; the girl caddie; the proud waiter; the treasure hunter; the perfectionist, the karaoke queen. Can't you just hear them?

When you look for a topic and write your essay, keep in mind how you will be dubbed. You want to be memorable!

This is how you do it: Hook the attention of that college admissions officer with a little story about "the time" you faced a problem, and then show him or her what you are made of by relating how you grappled with it and learned from it.

Sound simple? It is!

Step Four:
Fire It Up

QUICKIE: Here's the formula your essay will follow now that you have an anecdote to start with: You tell your mini-story that involves some type of "problem" in your introduction, and then you go on to discuss how you handled that problem (most likely using your defining quality), and what you learned in the process.

Make sure you do not try to impress with your story or essay by listing accomplishments; be careful of overly sensitive topics (death, divorce, illegal activity, etc.) and general, cliché topics (mission trips, life in the bubble, sports events or injuries, Harry Potter, how much you hate writing college essays, etc.)

Here are a couple examples of how your defining quality and

anecdote (with a problem) can line up in the form of an essay topic:

A. (Quality: humility) You are multi-talented and always excel at whatever you do—whether it's in school, sports or your favorite activity, drama. (Anecdote) You tell about "the time" you were so certain you would get the lead role in the school musical, (Problem) but learned it went to someone else. (Lesson Learned: You were devastated, but learned some valuable new skills and values by playing a secondary role.)

B. (Quality: respectful) You grew up in the south and always use formal manners. (Anecdote) You tell about "the time" you held a door open for a fellow female student after moving to Southern California (where it's uncool to use old-fashioned manners), and (Problem) how she reacted negatively and told you to "Get lost!" (Lesson Learned: You learned how to accept your differences and about how manners are really a form of respect.)

C. (Quality: problem-solver) You love learning how to tie knots. (Anecdote) You tell about "the time" you hoisted yourself high in a tree one day for fun, (Problem) and you got stuck. (Lesson Learned: You eventually got down, but learned how tying knots taught you how to think about resolving issues in your life.)

How to Find a Twist

Notice that another element of a good story or essay is "the unexpected." If you have some stories in mind, see if they include something the reader would not expect—about you or the experience. A little twist. Or surprise. These are easier to recognize in a story than come up with off the top of your head. But keep an eye out for this element in your stories. Readers love them.

One example of "the unexpected" was a news story years ago about how some pro football players were taking ballet lessons. Why was this story interesting? Because you would never expect a beefy football player to learn how to make graceful leaps across a room. The unexpected works like problems—they draw us in.

Most college admissions counselors advise their students to find topics that show colleges something they wouldn't learn about them in other parts of the application. Even better, I say, if your essay topic also shows them a side of you that they wouldn't expect.

HOT TIP: See if you have any interests and activities that people would not have expected you to care about. One of my students wrote about how he loved to bake cakes for his water polo team. The essay was great because it included this unexpected talent (not revealed in other parts of his application), and revealed another side to this athlete that was interesting and likeable.

One of my favorite essays was written by a student who was accomplished at everything—school, dance and social activities. But she had a secret passion. She loved the actor, Robert Patterson, from the *Twilight* series. Why would writing about such a mainstream topic be any good? Because her secret little crush was something we wouldn't have expected from such an over-achieving student. It revealed another side to her personality and actually made her seem more real, more likeable.

Now, before we go further, take a minute and skim through these general tips on what to avoid in an essay topic. Knowing what topics to steer clear of can clarify what makes a good topic. You can make almost any topic work, of course, but if you want to give yourself a break, stay away from these potential losers:

TOPICS TO AVOID

Listing accomplishments. Don't even think about just rattling off amazing things you have done, people you have met or places you have visited. Way too broad and boring! And bragging is not a good way to make friends.

Death, divorce, tragedies in general. It's not so much that these can be downers, but they're such powerful topics that they can be challenging to write about. (The "death" topic applies to family, friends and especially those beloved pets.)

That said, if you have experienced a huge loss in your life, and it completely turned your world upside down and changed you in a big way, please give it a shot. I have read some poignant essays about personal tragedies and intense issues. If nothing else, they show your grit, or raw determination to work through misfortune.

If you endured an alcoholic dad, or watched someone you love die from cancer or struggle with a chronic illness yourself, you almost have to write about these challenges. They can't help but define you in a big way. The key is to spend most of the essay talking about how you are dealing with the problem, and not overdramatizing the situation and your pain. Do your best to just tell it like it is.

"The most important thing/person in my life." Again, this is just too broad and loaded, whether you want to talk about God or your mom or your best friend. It's beautiful that you have these in your life, but they usually are boring to read about. The essay needs to be mainly about you.

Sports. The thrill of victory. Agony of defeat. Done. Dull. Avoid if possible. Especially sports injuries. (If there's a little "time," unexpected moment or incident that happened to occur while you were playing a sport, that can work. You just don't want to write about how you won the state championship, scored the winning goal or tore your ACL.)

Humor. Although a story you convey in one of your essays may be funny, do not try to be funny—there is a difference. Keep your delivery straight and just tell what happened. If your story has some funny parts to it, way to go. Self-deprecating humor (where you poke fun at yourself) seems to work best.

"I'm so lucky." Many college-bound students are privileged to live in beautiful, affluent towns and cities, and go on fun vacations, and that's great, lucky you. But talking about this can be a big turn-off. The last thing anyone wants to read about is your ski trip to Aspen or your hot oil massage at a fancy resort.

Do-good experiences. These can range from mission trips to Costa Rica to tutoring underprivileged kids through the local schools. Although essays can certainly involve these experiences, the topic needs to be on a specific experience within that broader trip or program. Zero in on a moment, not the whole experience. Essays that basically describe trips or volunteering are boring. Specific, unexpected things that happen during them, however, can be great topics!

Sensitive topics. Since you are writing for an audience who you want to like you, it's important to use your common sense in terms of topics that have a high tendency to make people angry or upset because they do not agree with your opinion. Politics and religion are particularly provocative. No matter what, don't preach about any topic.

The un-essay. Many students, often some of the brightest, have a fundamental reaction to these essays and the assignment to reveal yourself in 500 or 650 words. They want to get creative and in-your-face since that feels more genuine to them. They want to write in stream-of-consciousness or be sarcastic. I totally understand this reaction. However, you must remember your goal with these essays: to get accepted. Save the radical expression for after you get into college.

Illegal behavior. Drug use. Sexual activities. Arrests or jail time. Even if you stopped doing these illegal or unethical things, it's still not the best idea to bring them up here. If nothing else, the admissions folks might just wonder about your judgment in general for not steering clear of these topics.

As you can tell, I'm starting to use "times" and anecdotes interchangeably. This is because they end up being pretty much the same thing. Stick with me here—it will make more sense once you start writing.

Step Five:
Tell Your Story

QUICKIE: When you write your essay, stick with the past tense, write like you talk and avoid the standard 5-paragraph essay format. Start at the peak of the action or drama when writing your anecdote for the introduction; use descriptive details and the 5Ws; make the reader feel as though he or she was there.

You have found a story that you like and that relates to one of your core qualities. Now it's time to tell it. When writing your essay using a narrative style, here are a few basic rules:

Start with an anecdote. This is your mini-story describing an incident, moment or an exchange written creatively and in a condensed form. Often it only describes the most intense part of your story. This will be your introduction, and comprise the first paragraph, and possibly the second. See sample anecdotes starting on page 67.

HOT TIP: There is a huge difference between writing a story and using an anecdote. In these essays, you are not going to use the entire essay to tell a story. You are using only a piece of a story to start your essay—the anecdote.

Write in the first person. You will use "I" and "me" and "us," etc. Do not shift into "you."

Stick with past tense. When relating your story, tell it like it happened in the past, which it did. (Instead of "I walk" you will use "I walked".)

Ditch the 5-paragraph format. Your style will be less formal than most essays you are used to writing in English class. You will not use the classic 5-paragraph format. (We are going to use Show *and* Tell as our structure, which I will explain in Step 6.)

Write like you talk. The style is more casual, familiar, as though you are talking to someone you know. Think of a friendly adult, so you are informal, yet not quite as relaxed as with your best friends. A little jargon is okay, but keep it clean.

I'm always pretending that I'm sitting across from somebody. I'm telling them a story, and I don't want them to get up until I'm finished.   Writer James Patterson

Don't try to make it perfect. Just get something on paper. Then you can go back and polish it up later.

More Advice on How to Write an Anecdote

Once you have a little story to share, how do you start? Visualize the incident, exchange or moment you are going to describe. Instead of leading up to the moment, you want to start the story as close to the height of the drama, the climax of the little crisis or the second the pain or problem hit. In other words, try to begin your description at the peak of the action.

Here's an example of an anecdote from one of the best storytellers, humorist David Sedaris. This is how he started a piece for *The New Yorker* called "Turbulence":

On the flight to Raleigh, I sneezed, and the cough drop I'd been sucking on shot from my mouth, ricocheted off my folded tray table, and landed, as I remember it, in the lap of the woman beside me, who was asleep and had her arms folded across her chest. I'm surprised that the force didn't wake her—that's how hard it hit—but all she did was flutter her eyelids and let out a tiny sigh, the kind you might hear from a baby.

See how Sedaris described a simple moment? Notice the problem? How he began at the peak of the action, with barely any lead up or background? And something happened. Of course, he's a master writer and had a lot of practice crafting these, but you can write them, too. (See more sample anecdotes on page 67.)

In your anecdote, tell us quickly what happened, where it happened and who it involved. Use your descriptive language to help us visualize what took place. Use *descriptive details* to put us back in that moment: What did it look like, what did it smell or sound like, where and when was it happening? (In that first paragraph or two, we should know the 5Ws: Who, What, When, Where and Why.)

Here is an example of an anecdote describing a "time" or incident written by a high student for his college application essay:

I stood staring at the stacks of dishes, many covered with fish bones and dabs of mashed potato or a few leftover carrots. Waiters kept bringing in new loads, piling them by

31

the sink until there was no room left. Even though the kitchen exhaust fan roared, the place smelled of garlic, burnt grease and sweat.

"Out of the way, kid," said one waiter as he shoved through the swinging door. "Better get to work, the line's out the door."

*(**Background**) Although my father owns our Italian restaurant in my hometown, last summer was my first time helping in the kitchen. Usually, I just directed the overflow parking out back during the tourist crush. But about an hour earlier, my dad called, panicked, and told me his dishwasher had quit.*

See how the first couple paragraphs *show* "the problem"? It's a busy restaurant and there's no one to wash the dishes. Big problem. In the third paragraph, the writer give us a little more background—what led up to this moment or problematic event. Next, the writer can share how this whole catastrophe made him feel, and then develop his essay explaining how he dealt with it and what he learned.

By the end of an essay like this, we will get an idea about this writer, how he thinks about things, what he cares about, how he copes with stress, etc. In the process, the writer will reveal core qualities about himself, such as how he is a fast learner, has leadership qualities, or how he learned that he actually enjoys stepping into a chaotic situation and making it better.

This type of writing takes practice. But give it a try and you might surprise yourself. See how a little snippet of dialogue (talking) brings the scene to life? And how the details help you experience it: Don't just say the kitchen smelled bad, but give details about exactly what it smelled like and why.

Set the Scene

When writing an anecdote, you usually need to do a little setting of the scene. Paint the surroundings with words. Use what are called sensory details, those that rely on the five senses. See what details the writer used to set the kitchen scene:

- **What did it look like?** Piles of dirty dishes, stacked in sink, swinging door.
- **What did it sound like?** Kitchen fan roaring.
- **What did it smell like?** Garlic, burning grease, sweat.
- **What did it taste like?** No tasting in this one.
- **What did it feel like (emotionally):** This is where you use descriptive details to help us understand the heat of the moment.

Once you have set the scene, how do you convey the suspense, drama or tension in a problem? Descriptive details! Here's how the writer dropped in details to help us feel his pain:

The waiters "shoving through the swinging door." (Indicates stressed wait staff.)

The line is out the door. (It's a busy night; people waiting; building pressure.)

You are dazed at first. ("staring at the stack of dishes")

It's your "first time." (First times of anything are always stressful.)

Your dad called you, "panicked." (A panicked dad is not a good thing.)

Also, can you find the 5Ws in this anecdote? These are usually all we need to get a general idea of the context of your anecdote. These can be in the anecdote or in the backgrounding paragraph.

Who? You
What? Restaurant
When? Last summer
Where? Hometown
Why? Dad needed help

Start Your Anecdote in the Middle of the Action

Also, note how the writer doesn't build up to the incident, but starts in the middle of the action—and then gives some background in the third paragraph. This is the KEY to writing a powerful "hook" anecdote. Help your reader step right into the middle of the mess at the start of your essay.

Also, do you see how this is an everyday or "mundane" topic—washing dishes is not what you would call an "impressive" topic, yet it works well to showcase the writer's "impressive" qualities. I know it's difficult to trust me on this, but if you have a topic idea that you think is too common or unimpressive, think again. You actually might have hit on a good one!!

My advice at this point is to devote a half hour to writing up an anecdote. A half hour. That's nothing! If you write one you like, you are sure to *Escape Essay Hell!* That's the hardest part of all—finding a great topic and crafting a little introduction. The rest just falls in place. It doesn't have to be perfect, but don't read further until you've given it a shot.

HOT TIP: Once you have cranked out a little anecdote, give it a read. Chances are you could start even closer to the peak action. Try shaving off the first sentence or two and see if it reads even better. This doesn't always work, but often improves the anecdote immensely.

Step Six:
Add Structure

QUICKIE: In your essay, you will create a loose structure by both "showing" AND "telling." In your introduction, where you share a little story as an anecdote, you will be using details to "show" the story. When you go on to *explain* how you handled the problem and what you *learned* from it, you will be "telling." Hence, the Show *and* Tell formula.

After you write your anecdote, you will need to go back in time to put the little story in a larger context before you move forward. This is called "the back story." Also, show some emotion in your essay; include a little dialogue if it works; and, open up to make it compelling.

Let's say you have a good start and described a "problem," but aren't sure where to go from there. The next step—often in the second paragraph or so—is to back up a bit to "where it all started."

Since you started in the middle of a little story, you need to now step back in time and explain how you got to that point. It's called putting the anecdote in context.

Example of a Back Story

Say you wrote about the time you forgot your lines in the middle of the school play, and started your essay describing yourself up on stage, messing them up, and almost fainting. In the next paragraph, you need to back up and let the reader understand how you got to this point.

The paragraph after your anecdote could read something like this: *I first knew I wanted to be an actress when I dressed up like the lion in The Wizard of Oz in first grade. By high school, I started trying out for parts in the plays, and last year got the lead role in The Music Man...*

I like to tell my students to think about saying the words: "It all began when…" and go back as far as you need to, and quickly summarize events to bring the reader back up to the moment of your big problem. It might not always work this simply, but the idea is to provide enough background so that your anecdote makes sense.

The Magic Formula: Show *and* Tell

Now that you have an anecdote and back story, it's time to move forward into the meatier part of your essay. It helps here to understand how to structure a narrative essay.

Because the best college app essays are almost always

narrative, they are written in a looser, more conversational style. The structure also is more fluid. Try to forget about those more formal, five-paragraph essays that you were taught in your English classes.

To help you find a natural structure for your narrative essay, I encourage you to try the Show *and* Tell approach. There's a chance you might find this confusing because your English teacher always told you, when talking about how to write, to "Show, don't tell." This is not what I am talking about here. Although the "show" part is the same, the "tell" part is equally important in good writing.

Here's my attempt to help you understand the difference between "showing" and "telling," and then why you need both in your essay:

The Story of Spotty

Think back to your kindergarten days when you brought something from home to Show *and* Tell. You brought Spotty, your favorite stuffed animal dog. When you held up Spotty to show your classmates what he looked like, that was "showing." (In an essay, you would just describe what he looked like, felt like, smelled like, etc., with your descriptive words: He was stuffed, furry, black and white spots, smelled like an old blanket, etc.)

Then you had to "tell" about Spotty—why you chose him to bring, what he meant to you, how you got him (the "back story"), etc. Once you start *explaining* what Spotty meant to you, or how you felt about him, or what you learned, that is all "telling."

(Spotty's "back story" might start with: "My parents gave Spotty to me for my 6th birthday...")

The main idea behind shifting back and forth between "showing" and "telling" is that if you do either too long, you risk losing the reader's interest. Think about Spotty. If you just stood up there and showed everyone your stuffed animal, they might enjoy looking at him, but after a while they would want to know more about why you were displaying him. "So, you have a cool stuffed animal, but what about it?" they might think.

And if you didn't bring Spotty to show them, and just sat up there and explained why you loved your stuffed animal, they would grow bored very quickly, and want to see him for themselves.

When you write an anecdote, you are "showing" because you use descriptive details, sensory descriptions and scene-setting to help the reader "see" what you are talking about. But after you "show" the reader something, you then need to "tell" them what it means. You explain it, analyze it, reflect upon on it. That is called "telling."

HOT TIP: Know the difference between when you are "showing" and when you are "telling:

Showing = Providing concrete details, specific examples, telling a story, using dialogue, sensory descriptions, visuals, evidence, action. Everything that is more *specific* and *tangible*.

Telling = Explaining, reflecting, analyzing, interpreting, giving background, etc. Everything that is more *general* and *abstract*.

I love the simple question writer James Thayer asks in his little book about understanding the difference between showing and telling:

What's the difference between these two sentences?

His arm itches.

He scratched his arm.

Get it?

When a writer "shows" you details and you can "see" the point for yourself, you are more likely to also understand it.

To structure your narrative essay, I suggest you use just **one round** of "showing" and "telling." The Show *and* Tell approach. Start by "showing" with your anecdote, and then shift into "telling" when you explain and analyze the point of the anecdote. (In longer pieces, you shift back and forth between showing and telling to keep your reader engaged. But this essay is a shorter piece—average word count around 500 to 650—and we use the Show *and* Tell format to give the essay a basic structure.)

Here's a tiny outline of when you might Show *and* Tell in your essay:

> **Start** the essay with an anecdote, mini-story or vignette. **SHOW.**
> **Background** the introduction (the "back story"). **TELL.**
> **Explain** how you handled problem and reflect/analyze/share what you learned. **TELL.** (With "show" details sprinkled In wherever possible.)
> **Wrap it up** with conclusion. **TELL.**

Notice how this Show *and* Tell format is the opposite of those 5-paragraph essays from English class. In the 5-paragraph essay, you started by "telling" about your point by providing general background on the topic and including a main point, or thesis. Then you went on to provide specific examples to support your point, which was more like "showing."

In narrative essays, it's the opposite. Essayists almost always start with "showing." That way, you grab or "hook" the reader at the start. Then you shift into "telling" when you give background.

To further simplify, these essays are roughly one third Show, and the rest Tell. You might wonder: With all that abstract "telling" going on, how do you keep the reader's interest? Here are a couple other elements to consider adding after you start with your anecdote and shift into "tell" mode. These are simple techniques that can help connect with your reader to help them care about you and what you think.

*Don't **tell** me the moon is shining; **show** me the glint of the light on the broken glass.* Writer Anton Chekhov

The Big Tell

After you start with your anecdote, you give the "back story" and start explaining what it all means. Depending upon your story or topic, these suggestions might not all be relevant, so just use the ones that fit your essay:

Show Some Emotion

Once you told your anecdote, and then put it in context with some background (It all started…), you can pick up the story line to show us what happened next. If you started by describing a problem, now is the time to let us know how it all made you feel.

This is how we relate to your pain and understand why we should care about you and your problem. You don't need to overdo this part; just a quick sentence or two and we will get the idea. Think back to how you were feeling at the lowest point.

In the sample anecdote about the student thrown into a busy restaurant kitchen, he might have said, "I knew I was over my head." Or "I started feeling dizzy and almost bolted out the door."

Other ways to let the reader in on your emotional reaction to the problem: "I thought my world was over." "I thought my parents would kill me." "I felt like pulling the covers over my head and staying in bed for the rest of my life." "I felt trapped, as though I had no where to turn." "I never thought I would figure it out."

HOT TIP: Open up about yourself. When you reveal your inner thoughts and feelings, this helps the reader empathize with you—and makes you feel real and human. Showing vulnerability, self-doubt and authenticity takes a lot of courage. For college essays, that's good stuff, since it sets you apart from the crowd, forges a deeper connection with the reader and shows the maturity to be introspective and open.

Include Dialogue

If you didn't include any dialogue—quoting yourself or someone else—in your anecdote, you might consider dropping in a line or two when you background your story. You can use it to add drama to your story, such as a snippet from a key player in the story, or even quote yourself.

Describing your inner dialogue or thoughts, or even those of others in the story, is one of the best ways to give your essay that "narrative" style and tone. Usually you only need a few words, or a short line or two. Dialogue makes the essay read more like a novel or short story (fiction!), even though it's true.

If it was something you thought, just let the reader know that. Example: "You are never going to reach the top of that mountain," I thought to myself while looking up the steep cliff.

Example: "Why do I always chicken out at the last minute?" I asked myself.

One general rule about dialogue, which applies to narrative essays, is to start a new paragraph every time someone *new* says something.

HOT TIP: Another trick to writing dialogue is to try to compress it. Once you write a couple sentences, or a quick exchange between yourself and someone else, try cutting it down. Usually, you can get the point across with fewer words than you think, and they end up snappier sounding, too.

If you are using dialogue—say it aloud as you write it. Only then will it have the sound of speech.   Writer John Steinbeck

Be Specific

When you are in "telling" mode, one way to keep your essay interesting is to continue to sprinkle in some of those "show" details and examples. When you use a word, see if you can get even more specific.

SUPER HOT TIP: If you mention a pet, use its name. If you mention sneakers, name the brand. Not just a "car," but the year, color and make. If you mention a song, include the title. This will help bring color and interest to all parts of your essay. Nothing else will spice up your story better than these types of details.

Check out the details in this passage from The Office writer and actress Mindy Kaling, who described a cliché archetype for female actresses. In a *New Yorker* magazine piece about women in the movies, she calls this character The Ethereal Weirdo. Notice all the details, which I will bold:

"This girl can't be pinned down and may or may not show up

when you make concrete plans with her. She wears **gauzy blouses** and **braids**. She likes to **dance in the rain** and she weeps uncontrollable if she sees **a sign for a missing dog or cat**. She might **spin a globe**, place her finger on a random spot, and decide to move there...If (The Ethereal Weirdo) were from real life, people would think she was a **homeless woman** and **cross the street** to avoid her."

This description is funny because you can picture and recognize this type of girl from the visual images and specific details. If you are describing someone or something, always try to help the reader see what you see—and chances are they also will feel what you feel. Which is even better. (Also, notice how Mindy writes like she talks. That is the "voice" you are after in your essay.)

Back Up Your Points, Declarations or Observations With Examples

When you are in "telling" mode, and starting to analyze your actions or thoughts, you can power your writing by backing up your points with specific examples. Real-life examples snap your reader out of the (sometimes dull) abstract language and back into your piece.

Example: (Telling) *When I thought about my reaction to that chaotic scene in the restaurant, I realized that I have a pattern to handling crises. At first, I go into panic mode and almost freeze with anxiety. (Showing with an example)* **It felt like the time my Irish Setter, Sandy, darted into traffic and was hit by a delivery truck.** *I just stood there, as though my legs had turned to stone...*

HOT TIP: See how a real-life example pulls you back into the essay? In this case, the example was also a comparison (It felt *like*...). Remember how using a simile can brighten your writing with a creative comparison (using "like" or "as")? See if you can use at least one of these writing devices in your essay to give it some texture and color.

Look For the Larger Metaphors

When you are trying to bring depth to your essay, the use of a metaphor can work magic. A metaphor is when you express one thing in terms of something else. (The trapdoor of depression. Dad was a rock. The winds of change.) In these essays, one trick is to look at the problem you described in your anecdote and see if it could be extended from a specific, literal problem into a larger, abstract one.

Example: The dishwasher who faced the out-of-control kitchen. Literal problem: lack of order in the restaurant kitchen. Figurative problem: chaos in life situations. So when the writer reflected on how he handled the kitchen problem, he could extend that moment into how he handles chaos in a broader sense, maybe in other parts of his life or thinking.

Another Example: The girl who messed up her lines in the school play. Literal problem: flubbing her lines on stage. Figurative problem: how to recover your poise in real life, on the stage of life.

The idea is that you explore in your essay how a small issue can be interpreted into a higher, more abstract level, and that if you are able to see that, you can learn on a deeper level as well.

Never use a metaphor, simile, or other figure of speech which you are used to seeing in print. Writer George Orwell.

In other words, if you sling around similes or metaphors, make up your own. If you use ones you have heard before, they will sound cliché.

Step Seven:
Explain What You Learned

QUICKIE: After you write your anecdote, and background it, you need to explain how you dealt with the problem, and what you learned from it. Include what you learned about yourself, about others and the world. Look for the universal truth in your essay to add depth.

You have relayed your anecdote, provided background and shared your reaction to it. Now it's time to get a grip. You are clearly going to shift away from "showing" into "telling" mode at this point, but like I said, it's fine if you slip in some of those "showing" details here and there.

In general, you will now explain how you handled the problem, and what you learned in the process. Toss in a conclusion, and you will be almost out of Essay Hell!

Your Recovery

Let's say you relayed some type of problem (challenge, obstacle, fear, flaw, crisis, etc.), and you are not feeling good about, in fact, you might be upset and freaked out. What we want to know next is how you faced it, and turned things around.

By the third or fourth paragraph, start to tell us how and why you were able to recover from this problem, or challenge, experience, obstacle or mistake. This is the most important part of your essay—assuming you hooked your reader with a juicy problem at the beginning. What did you do to handle this problem? What steps did you take? What did you think about or draw upon to change your thinking or actions to get back on course?

Share your "thought-process" by stepping us through with you: "First, I did this…then, I remembered this, and then I went on to do this. Finally, this happened…" (Stick to chronological order at this point.)

HOT TIP: Remember, you did not have to totally solve the problem—it can be fine if you just found a way to handle it or deal with it. If you had a fear of heights as a problem, you didn't have to totally get over that fear—just share what you did to cope or handle it in your life.

Share What You Learned

By now, you have explained what steps you took to deal with

or handle or fix your problem. It's time to dig deeper and let us know what you learned from that experience. Or another way to put it: How were you affected or changed?

You don't just want to say what you learned, but also delve into how you learned it. To flush out some ideas, start with these three points:

What did you learn about yourself?

What did you learn about others?

What did you learn about life, or the world?

Usually when you handle or address a problem—including an obstacle, a personal flaw, a challenge, a crisis, etc.—you need to find some source of inspiration or help in dealing with it. Where did you look to find help or support or inspiration in handling your problem? An inspiring quote? A wise friend? Something you learned from a previous experience? Include this in your explanation.

Also, many times in dealing with a problem, you also had to change something about yourself, most commonly how you think about something. This is a very rich source of fodder you can include in your essay, to flush out your ideas and reveal how you think and what you care about. It often touches on your most basic values—as well as your defining qualities.

Here are some other ways to express what you learned:

I never thought about it before, but now I believe that...

When I looked back at what happened, I realized that...

It took me a while, but after talking about it with my

friends, I saw things differently. Now I think that...

For the first time, I started to wonder about...

Things slowly started to change. I began to notice that...and realize that...and care about...

At first, it seemed as though nothing had changed. But then I started to understand that...

If something changed along the way—how you think about things, what you care about or value, what you now would do differently—include those thoughts and feelings. This is your chance to reflect, to explain, to analyze what happened, and share what you learned. Yes, this is the main "telling" part.

HOT TIP: The best way to make this part of the essay compelling is to try to be open and direct about yourself and thinking. Remember, you don't have to come across as superman or superwoman to solve your problem. You are only human, and most likely just getting started in your adult life. So it's fine to not know everything or have all the answers.

I find when writers share some of their self-doubts it actually makes them very likeable, and I trust them more. It's easier to relate to what they are going through and telling us. So don't aim for perfection; aim for the truth.

For instance, it's fine to say something about your self-doubts or worries. Here's how a writer could inject that slightly confessional tone into the essay about the restaurant:

*After I calmed down and got a plan on how to attack the chaos and mess in my dad's kitchen, I started to realize that I was good at these pressure-cooker situations. **I can't say we still didn't mess up some major orders that night, or that we left the place spotless**, but at least I learned how a level head and a sound strategy could save the day....*

48

See how we almost like this guy better because he was a big enough person not to claim that he made everything perfect? A little self-questioning or doubt can go a long way in making sure an essay about yourself doesn't cross that fine line into bragging or chest-pounding.

The Power of a Universal Truth

Here's another tip on how to take your essay to a deeper level. It's called finding the "universal truth" in your piece. A universal truth is the same thing as a life lesson—it's something that is true for almost everyone. Usually they are very simple, and almost cliché. Examples: No pain, no gain. Sometimes you have to fail to succeed. Cheaters never win. Bigger is better. Everyone loves a winner. You don't always get what you want. It's darkest before the dawn.

In almost any story, there's a universal truth, or simple life lesson or moral. See if you have one in your story. You don't have to quote the little life lesson, but you might want to touch upon it in your own words. "Sometimes in life, you have to face your fears." Or "In life, it's necessary to make mistakes to learn."

Step Eight:
Focus Your Point

QUICKIE: Even though these essays are written in a looser style, you want to be able to focus your message with one main point. And that main point needs to be about you! See if you can state in one sentence how your anecdote connects to or illustrates your defining quality.

If you have chosen an anecdote that relayed a problem, and shared how you handled it and what you learned, take a minute to check if you can summarize what you have just revealed about yourself. Chances are, it will highlight one of your defining qualities.

Here's an example of how an essay could unfold:

Say you picked being "determined" as a defining quality. And being "under 5 feet tall" as your problem. In order to show the reader this problem, you started with "a time" that being short was a problem and then went into how your determination helped you deal with it.

You started with "a time" when you had to clear the high jump in order for your track team to win an important meet. You started your anecdote by describing yourself the moment before you made the big jump.

Sample Outline

Introduction (Anecdote) (The strike out line below shows how you can often take out/edit a first line or two and improve your introduction.)

As I stared at the blue pole in front of me, I focused on an invisible point about a foot above it. Ignoring my shaking legs, I counted down to myself, and then bolted toward the bar. All I thought about was jumping, and pushing every atom in my body toward the sky. After landing on the pad, I shut my eyes and listened for the sound of the pole rattling to the ground. (Problem: needs to clear the bar.)

Back Story (It all started...)

As a teenage boy who had yet to pass 5 feet, most of my friends and even my parents tried to discourage me from picking the high jump as my main sport in track my freshman year of high school. **(Inject how the problem made you feel)** *I never let on how much their negative comments stung, and always just laughed off their doubts and unwanted opinions. As someone with the nickname of "Shrimp," I thought this was a chance to change my image.*

Handling the Problem

Here you could talk about why joined you the team, how you weren't very good at first, how you practiced in your backyard and rigged up your own vault, spent hours jumping, read all the tips, etc. You slowly got better, surprising coach and yourself. But how you never expected that one day the status of the team would depend upon your clearing a six-foot high jump.

What You Learned

I still feel lucky that I never nicked the pole on that day, and the bar stuck and we won the meet. It was my highest jump ever, and I'm not sure I will ever be able to repeat it. But that doesn't matter. I learned more than just how to jump like a kangaroo during those years in track. I learned how I didn't have to let others define who I was, and that if I set a goal, and found my own skills and strategy to meet it, I could be who I wanted.

(Did you catch the universal truth in that last sentence? What he meant, in a nutshell, was that, "In life, if you are determined, you can do almost anything." He broadened the idea of how he was determined to clear the high jump to the idea that he can also "clear" other obstacles in life with the same core value: determination.)

Conclusion

(Bring reader up to present) *I still love the high jump. There are now other guys who can jump higher than me. And I may never clear six feet again. But I will always feel like a tall guy for other reasons. I know I can always rise above almost any challenge by drawing on my wits and determination ...*

In this essay, you can summarize the main point this guy was making about himself by plugging in his defining quality, his problem and how it affected him:

52

"I'm the kind of person who is **determined** (defining quality), because when I encountered friends and family trying to limit my abilities due to my **short height** (problem), I learned that I **could clear almost any obstacle in my life**—whether it was a high bar or people trying to tell me what I can't achieve."

In effect, this is your main point. And you are going to use your essay to illustrate and explain it.

HOT TIP: After you relay your anecdote, you may want to work in some other smaller examples to further "prove" your main point in other areas of your life. This is an opportunity to weave in your other related interests, accomplishments, and activities where you used your defining quality in a natural, meaningful way. For example, if you say you are a problem-solver, work in some other examples of occasions when you have solved problems.

Step Nine:
Wrap It Up

QUICKIE: In your conclusion, try to bring the reader up to present time regarding the problem you described in your anecdote. Also, restate your main point—what you learned from facing this problem. End on a broad, positive note, and address how you hope to apply what you learned in your future. A snappy last sentence always helps.

Like all conclusions, you are basically wrapping up your story, summing up your main point(s) and ending on a broad, upbeat note. You can mix it up however you want, but here are some surefire ways to making it a memorable wrap:

Bring Your Essay Full Circle

Find a way to link back to that original anecdote you started with. Bring the reader up to date to the present. For instance, with the high jumper, here's how he could let us know where he is with that sport now:

I'm not sure if I will continue high jumping in college, and it's not a sport you can pick up and play anywhere. So there's a chance I may never catapult myself over a pole again in the near future. But I will never forget that moment of exhilaration as I cleared that bar during our big meet. Everyone raced up and gave me high fives and big hugs. What I will always remember is that feeling of rising above all the opinions of other people who thought I was just another short guy...

Most of your essay was telling about something that happened in the **past**, and now in your conclusion you have brought them into the **present** by linking to your beginning–which poises you to mention your **future** aspirations in the last sentence or two.

Here are some other examples of linking back to the introduction or beginning anecdote. Notice how each one brings the reader up to date with how you are doing now in regards to the story, moment or experience you shared in your essay:

- If you started by describing a time you got stuck in a tree because of a tangled rope, bring that experience up to date in the conclusion: "I haven't climbed many trees lately, but I **still** love practicing tying knots. And recently, my knots have helped me solve problems in my life..."

- If you started by describing a poignant moment with someone you lost or who was battling illness, you could bring the reader up to speed by talking about how you are doing **now**: "I still think about my dad more times than I can count during the day, and I miss him with all my heart, but that raw, aching grief is starting to calm down a bit...."

- If you started with an anecdote about a time a fellow water polo player avoided you, apparently because your enormous size made him assume you were a mean guy, link back to that moment and tell us how things are going for you **today**: "When I walk into a room full of strangers, I will always spot that kid who looks at me with a hint of fear. And that might never change. I will always tower over most of my friends, and I actually enjoy trying to make others comfortable. But I'm a big guy, and I have learned how to also be a big person..."

Also in your conclusion, you can re-state your main point in a fresh way, and touch on your core quality and what you learned, if possible: "At this point, I almost believe that if I'm determined enough, I just might grow another inch or two." (Humor never hurts in these essays; it often shows you don't take yourself too seriously.)

End by touching on how you intend to use the life lesson from your essay in your future plans, to meet goals or dreams: "If nothing else, I'm eager to find out exactly how high I can go with my dream of finding a career in the world of chemistry or engineering.

HOT TIP: It's always a good idea to try to end with a little "kicker" sentence—if it works and doesn't sound too corny. Don't be afraid to be idealistic and declare your dreams or goals. Or you can try a play on words. If you aren't sure your "kicker" works or not, have a friend or parent give you some feedback. "One thing for sure, I know I won't come up short." Hmmm. Does that work or is it too corny?

I would not move forward with these steps unless you have zeroed in on a good topic—one with a little story (anecdote), a defining quality and a problem. You can either write it all out in the form of a rough draft, or jot down the steps in an outline.

Here's a little guide if you want a format to follow:

Introduction
Anecdote: Mini-Story: Problem

Back Story
Give context to the anecdote: "It all started…": Then quickly bring the reader up to speed on the current problem. Go from there. Share how the problem made you feel.

Handling The Problem
Explain what steps you took to deal with the problem. Include: How you thought about it. When and why you got a plan or the strength to face the problem. What steps you took in handling it. How they worked out.

Lessons Learned
What did you learn by handling this problem? Include: What you learned about yourself, about others and about the world or life in general. (Touch on a "universal truth.")

Conclusion
Link back to the anecdote and bring your reader up to current time in regard to the problem. Then, re-state the main point you are making with this essay about yourself—what you learned in dealing with this problem, how it changed you and/or your thinking about the world, what defining quality you used. End with how you will use what you learned in your future endeavors.

Step Ten:
Make It Perfect

QUICKIE: After you have a rough draft pounded out, go back and read it. If it bogs down, then make changes. Keep what you like. See where you can get more specific; use colorful details and examples to back up your points. Follow my editing checklist below.

By this point, you either need to spend time and go back over the first nine steps out of Essay Hell, and start writing, or you have a rough draft in hand. If you have a rough draft, congratulations, that's the hardest part! If you still need to write, remember what writer Anne Lamott said about first drafts: They need to be "shitty." That doesn't mean you are supposed to try to write a "shitty" first draft; it means not to worry too much if your first draft isn't perfect.

The goal is just to get out your messy ideas, points, words, whatever, so you can then go back and fix them up. It helps to map out your essay at first, which will make it easier when you go back to edit. It doesn't need to be a fancy, complicated outline, just make a numbered list of the basic points you want to cover in a certain order.

Look back in Step 9 and work off that mini-outline and write something about each number, then put it all together, and I bet you have a very decent rough draft.

Be Your Own Editor

When you go back and read your rough draft, listen to the points that you like (and keep those!) and pay attention to parts that are confusing or drag on (and change those.) Cut the longer parts first—an entire paragraph that you don't need, for instance—then go back and trim phrases or words. That's called editing.

I try to leave out the parts that people skip.   Writer Elmore Leonard

Trust yourself here. If relating your anecdote in your introduction takes up too much space in your essay, find parts that you can take out and still have your story make sense. This takes practice, but you will be surprised how good you get at it!

Stick the Word Count

My advice on word count restrictions on the college applications is to always, no matter what, stick to the limits—or keep them under. Never go over. Why would you want these admissions officers to think that you can't follow the simplest instructions? No matter how brilliant you think your essay is, chances are it only gets better when it's shortened. That's just the nature of good writing. The word count of 500 is a tough number to fit in everything, but the new Common App. 650-word length gives you plenty of room to strut your stuff. Age-old writing trick: Write long, then cut.

Here are some other narrative writing tips that can make your essay sing:

Vary your sentence length. If you have several long ones, make sure to pop in a short one. This always picks up the tempo of your piece. Readers are always grateful.

Go easy on the adverbs (-ly) and adjectives. If you use too many descriptors, they start to lose their power. Instead, try to pick the right noun and strong action verbs.

Use the thesaurus. Many writing experts warn young writers against relying on the thesaurus. I believe it can be a great help, if used correctly. Don't look up synonyms in order to find bigger, more impressive words for what you want to say. Do use it to find the exact right word (especially action verbs) or other ways to say the same thing.

Write like you talk. Resist shifting into that voice that is trying too hard to sound smart. Read your essay and if it sounds like you are forcing long words that you normally wouldn't use, or back into sentences with the passive voice, change them to sound more like you talk in real life.

If it sounds like writing, I rewrite it.   Writer Elmore Leonard

FINAL CHECKLIST (Your essay may not answer all these questions, but it should cover most of these points):

Your Topic

Does it have the unexpected?

Is it mundane?
Does it involve one of your defining qualities?
If you have an area of study you hope to pursue in college, does it relate to that? (Example: You want to be an engineer. Does your topic share a story that shows a defining quality that would make you a good engineer? Such as being a problem-solver, or logical thinker, or a fix-it guy?)

Introduction

Does it grab the reader?
Did you include details and specifics, not generalities.
Do you show us something instead of tell us about it.
Did it start in the middle of the action?
Do you have the 5Ws. The Who, What, When, Where, and Why?
Did you work in a snippet of dialogue?
Did you describe the setting of your problem with descriptive, sensory details?

Back Story

Do we understand the context of the anecdote you are telling?
If you didn't cover the 5Ws in the anecdote, did you fill us in here?
Do we have an idea where this essay is headed?
Did you include a line or two that shared how you felt about the problem or issue?
Do we feel your pain?

Handling the Problem

Did you explain what steps you took to deal with the problem?
Did you share how you thought about it, and your thought-process?
Did you take us through the steps in an order that makes sense?

Can you work in any other specifics about yourself or experience that helped you deal with this?

Lessons Learned

What did you learn from this experience?
Did this process reveal one of your core/defining qualities—either that you used or developed further or discovered along the way?
Were you changed in any way?
Did you mention what you learned about yourself?
Did you mention what you learned about others?
Did you mention what you learned about life in general, or how the world works? (A universal truth?)

Conclusion

Do you link back somehow to your introduction?
Do you re-state the main point you are making about yourself in fresh language?
Do you say how you will apply what you learned to future endeavors?
Do you end on a broad, upbeat note, and project your hopes and dreams into the future?

Other Points to Check

- Read your prompt (the question) one more time. Often a prompt will ask you to answer more than one question, or address several points.

- Stick to the word count. There's no reason to go over.

- Print out your essay and proofread it on paper. Often, errors pop out better in print than on the computer screen.

- Use common language and avoid using SAT vocab words that only some people know. Plethora, sycophant, fecund and phlegmatic, to name a few. If you don't use a word in normal conversation, don't force it in a narrative essay.

- Do you come across as competent, talented, insightful, etc.—but also humble and likeable? Often, tweaking how you say something about yourself, especially when talking about an accomplishment, can make all the difference.

- Check for common editing errors that spellcheck often doesn't catch—such as the proper use of it's and its/there, their and they're/your and you're.

- Read your essay several times before you send it. Get away from it for a day or two, and then read it with a fresh eye. Even better, have someone read it out loud to you.

Congratulations! You should have a completed college admissions essay, or a personal statement. If you are debating whether to include a title, read the following Bonus Chapter.

Optional Step:
Add a Title

I like titles. But they need to be good. A title should be short and witty. Not cutesy. The tone of the title and essay should match. The best ones don't give away too much about the essay, and only hint at what's to come. Do not use questions. And don't even think about a title that sounds anything like "My College Admissions Essay."

Now, how do you think of a title, a good title? Brainstorm ideas by playing off words that link to your theme, message or topic.

Example: A student wrote an essay about how he broke his wrist playing football, and how he learned more about the game sitting on the bench that season. Theme: How bad things can result in good things/How you can learn from a new perspective. (This "theme" is also a universal truth or "life lesson".)

Make a quick list of words from the essay that you could play around with: break, benched, football, sports, view, injury, hurt, new perspective…Let yourself "free associate," which means you list key words and sayings that come to mind when you say one of them, such as "break." Try the word in different tenses, in common phrases, in pop culture phrases (titles of movies, books, songs, etc.) and even clichés can work.

Also, skim your essay for catchy phrases that might work. Try mixing up a couple keys words to make your own phrase. You can also use the Internet to brainstorm ideas–just Google your keywords or phrases. Have fun with it.

Breaking Away (movie title)

Breaking Bad

The Big Break

Breaking Up

Break Out

You Deserve a Break Today (line from McDonald's commercial)

An Unexpected Break

Give Me A Break

A Break from the Past

Beyond the Break

I guess my favorite is Beyond the Break because it implies the metaphorical movement beyond the injury. But if I didn't like that one, I would move on to another key word. Keep playing around with them. Make a list. Read them out loud. One word will spark another and so on. You will know almost immediately when you hit on the right one.

If you can't find one you like, just skip it. Better no title than a bad title for your college application essay—unless one is requested or required.

Sample Anecdotes

I talked a lot about the power of starting a narrative essay with an anecdote, mainly in Chapter 5. In the examples below, notice how most or all of them were about mundane (ordinary/everyday) topics, involving some type of "problem." Also, how they used strong verbs and strands of dialogue, set the scene using sensory details and wrote in the past tense. Above all, something happened.

Some were a little fun or silly. Others sad or poignant. Most described a moment that lasted only a matter of minutes.

The writers also didn't give away everything in the first sentence or two—they made you wait and earn it. They relayed these mini-stories to *show* the reader something about themselves, as opposed to telling about or explaining it. That's why they grab the readers so well.

The best part of anecdotes is that they draw you into the essay and make you want to keep reading. See for yourself in these sample anecdotes from some of my former students' essays:

Trash Talk

We were about eight blocks from my house on our way to get fish tacos when I spotted the sign in the corner of my eye.

"Stop the car!" I shouted. My friend, who was driving, slammed on the brakes, then backed up. My eyes didn't deceive me: The hand-written sign read "Free Trampoline."

Some people might think a rusty, 10-year-old trampoline wouldn't be worth dragging home. But to me, it was almost too good to be true. Ever since I can remember, I have loved turning other people's trash into my personal treasures. ...

Regret

While eating my lunch and watching massive waves crash onto the sand last summer, I noticed two men lugging their heavy diving gear to the shoreline.

"Are they out of their minds, or could they be ex-Marines and know what they are doing?" I remember questioning myself. Although I was an off-duty lifeguard at the time, rather than asking if they were aware of the hazardous conditions, I sat and watched them gear up and enter the water.

That was a mistake that I regret to this day. ...

Fashionista

Cupping my daily steaming cup of espresso, I stared into the depths of my closet. After a few minutes, I stepped into a black fringe leather skirt, and pulled on my favorite knit sweater in rich burgundy. After slipping on a pair of grey suede ankle boots, I looked in the mirror, and cocked my head.

"Hmm, you can do better," I thought to myself, not quite happy yet. I added a gold collared necklace and grabbed a stack of chunky, vintage bracelets, wrapped my curls in a silky Prada scarf and tossed on an oversized military jacket. I made a final happy twirl in the mirror, and dashed out the door. ...

The Commute

As my mom backed out of our driveway, I glanced at the back seats to make sure my basketball gear was there, along with my school books, phone charger, and beat-up copy of Catch 22. We slowly wound through my neighborhood and over about a half dozen speed bumps, then pulled onto the highway heading south with the other Sunday traffic.

I sat back and watched the familiar landmarks flash past my window—the large Denny's sign with the missing "N," the large stretch of undeveloped land and the Coca Cola billboard that meant we were almost there.

I've made this 20-mile trip between my parents' homes for the last decade, ever since they divorced when I was seven. I never counted, but I must have taken it more than a thousand times. …

Stay Calm

Lying on the gurney in the hospital waiting room, I twisted and turned to try to relieve the jabs of pain under my ribs. The doctor told me my spleen had burst. Despite my agony, I was able to see the other patients lying on stretchers on either side of me, as many as ten in a row looking like something out of a Hollywood ER movie. Some were crying. A few were moaning. The guy next to me looked as though someone had filleted his face.

"Just keep breathing," I told myself, trying not to panic. After about a half hour, I calmed myself down and turned to the one thing that always seemed to get me through a hard time. I started to sing. …

Leaving Home

When my sister and I came home, the first thing we did was figure out where our mom was. The signs were there. It was after dark. She wasn't in the kitchen or living room. And I immediately spotted the empty bottle of wine on the counter.

"Stay away from mom, she's been drinking," I warned my younger sister. But moments later, my mom found us out back and started one of her typical rants. She started yelling at us for no apparent reason, and after threatening us with all types of punishment, she hurled a large trash can at me. It slammed against my arm and side. Feeling the pain, I remember thinking to myself that this was crazy, and I had to get out there. …

Selling Shoes

As I was arranging one of the shoe displays, I heard her patent leather heels clicking up the sidewalk before I saw her. Decked in diamonds from head to toe, the woman clutched her Yorkie in her Louis Vuitton tote, and strutted through the front door.

"Now don't assume she will be a snob," I thought to myself. But after our first encounter, it became clear this woman was as high maintenance as the price tag on her clothing. …

The Grill Master

The smoke was almost blinding. Grease spattered my face. It was a hot summer night, and the HOT grill almost topped out at 500 degrees. As sweat trickled down my back, I heard my ravenous friends starting to complain. I slathered another coat of marinade on the steaks, flipped the chicken wings and rolled the hot dogs a notch.

Some people would do almost anything to avoid the sweaty heat of the grill and pressure to produce a savory meal for their friends and family. Not me. Ever since eight grade and I could safely operate a large gas grill, I've been the one responsible for the meat. Whether it's a barbeque at the beach of a sit down meal for a half-dozen good friends, I'm the one standing to the side, out of reach of the conversation, standing alone by the flames. …

The Big Meanie

While grabbing lunch between games at a water polo tournament, I noticed one of my new teammates rarely looked me in the eye. Instead of taking the empty seat next to me, he opted to sit across the table. Even when I tried to start a conversation with him, he only looked down, and mumbled, "Oh, hey," and walked away.

This type of cold-shoulder treatment wasn't new to me. I'm a big guy. In bare feet, I'm about 6 feet 7 inches tall, and I'm pushing 300 pounds. Yes, it can be a pain. I bump my head going through doorways, I don't fit in most mid-size cars and clothes shopping can be a nightmare. But I understand that the world is made for average-sized people, and I'm above average. One thing, however, is hard for me to take: People who don't know me assume I'm mean. ...

Music Man

Sitting on an old couch in my friend's garage last year, I mentioned that I had produced my first song. When they asked me to play it, I plugged in my iPod, hit play and turned up the volume. Within seconds, they started laughing.

"Turn it off," one of them yelled.

Although I tried not to let it show, I felt a little humiliated. Even though this was my first attempt using professional software to make a hip-hop instrumental, I thought my piece was pretty good. Instead of calling it quits, I just grew more determined. I was not going to let any type of teasing or other detractors stop me from producing music. ...

Tied Up in Knots

Dangling about 30 feet above the ground, I looked down on the entire neighborhood park with its rolling hills, vibrant green grass, and tall eucalyptus trees. Buckled tightly in my brand new Diamond Mountain climbing harness, I admired my handiwork. My old blue and black braided climbing rope thrown over a branch held me aloft, while a slipknot I tied while hoisting myself up prevented my descent.

After a few minutes, I decided to return to the ground, but realized my knot grew too tight for me to untie. I was stuck.

Every since my dad taught me the Bowline in second grade, the intricacy of knots has fascinated me. ...

A Groupie

When my friend texted me that she was already at my front door for our study group, I leaped up onto my bed. In one pass, I ripped down the giant poster of Robert Patterson gazing out from above my pillow, shooting pushpins in every direction. Next, I scrambled over to my desk, and snatched the Edward and Bella dolls, pristine in their unopened plastic cases, and tossed them behind the couch. Finally, in one swoop, I gathered the pictures, buttons, cards, books and other Twilight Saga memorabilia off my shelf and buried them deep inside my sock drawer.

Moments before my friend burst into my room, I made one last glance for any overlooked signs of my deep dark secret: I am a Twilight junkie. ...

Two Moms

Sitting in my freshman Spanish class, I listened as the teacher turned the conversation to our families. He started asking each student about their parents, both their mother and father. I felt a familiar sense of dread and anxiety deep in my stomach. But I was ready for my turn.

"Que haces tu padre?" he asked me in Spanish, meaning, "What does your father do?"

As calmly and directly as I could, I explained to him in Spanish that I did not have a father because I have two mothers. They are lesbians. ...

Neat Freak

First, I plucked each of my eight pillows off my twin bed, and carefully stacked them on the hardwood floor from largest to smallest. Continuing my routine, I scooted the bed approximately two inches from the turquoise wall and tucked in each layer of bedding. Finally, I arranged two solid green pillows in the left corner of the bed, and propped my favorite flimsy pillow at the head of the white, chipping headboard. There. Done. Perfect. I walked over to the other end of my room, flipped off the lights, walked back to my perfectly coiffed bed, and climbed in.

To most people, making your bed before going to sleep seems crazy. But for me, growing up in a messy, chaotic family of six, I felt it was the only way to stay sane. ...

Window Dressing

Standing by the display window, I wrapped my arms around Sarah's slippery waist, struggling as I pulled the sheer, black turtleneck over one arm. As I yanked the sweater over her other arm, I heard a snap. One of her fingers dropped to the ground. Although Sarah and the store's other two mannequins were both relatively new, it has always been a battle to constantly change the mannequins and keep them fashionable. Needless to say, I was not looking forward to the skinny jeans.

Still, I knew that working at this small boutique in my hometown presented a unique opportunity for me. ...

Now Do You Get It?

I hope you understand now how you can turn any moment, incident or interaction into a lively, interesting-to-read, true-life mini-story. Now take a stab at writing one of these yourself! Anecdotes take practice, but you will love the end result. And so will your readers!

About the Author

Janine Robinson is a freelance writer and editor who lives in Laguna Beach, California. For the last six years, she has worked with college-bound students on their college application essays. Janine writes the popular blog, Essay Hell, which is filled with advice, tips and inspiration on how to write these dreaded essays.

For the last two decades, Janine has worked for top newspapers, magazines and Internet companies as both a writer and editor. She worked as a staff reporter on The Miami Herald and Orange County Register newspapers, edited a monthly lifestyle magazine for women, and worked as a writer and editor for several Internet-based education and news sites. Janine also holds a credential to teach high school English.

She helped her own two children escape Essay Hell. Her daughter—the first student she helped with a college application essay in 2008—recently graduated from a wonderful liberal arts college in the south with a double major in art and sociology, and her son is pursuing engineering at another fabulous college in the Pacific Northwest.

To escape Essay Hell, Janine enjoys hiking, yoga, surfing, gardening and birding.

For more advice and tips on how to escape essay hell, visit my web site: **www.EssayHell.com**.

Best of Luck!

Made in the USA
San Bernardino, CA
27 June 2015